YOUR KNOWLEDGE HAS VALUE

- We will publish your bachelor's and master's thesis, essays and papers

- Your own eBook and book - sold worldwide in all relevant shops

- Earn money with each sale

Upload your text at www.GRIN.com
and publish for free

Kalaiselvi N. Joshi, A. Sivasankari, S. Sudarvizhi

Performance Analysis of Proactive Reactive and Hybrid Routing Protocols Considering Link SNR Value Using Qualnet

GRIN Publishing

Bibliographic information published by the German National Library:

The German National Library lists this publication in the National Bibliography; detailed bibliographic data are available on the Internet at http://dnb.dnb.de .

Imprint:

Copyright © 2014 GRIN Verlag GmbH
Print and binding: Books on Demand GmbH, Norderstedt Germany
ISBN: 978-3-656-72315-8

This book at GRIN:

http://www.grin.com/en/e-book/278251/performance-analysis-of-proactive-reactive-and-hybrid-routing-protocols

GRIN - Your knowledge has value

Since its foundation in 1998, GRIN has specialized in publishing academic texts by students, college teachers and other academics as e-book and printed book. The website www.grin.com is an ideal platform for presenting term papers, final papers, scientific essays, dissertations and specialist books.

Visit us on the internet:

http://www.grin.com/

http://www.facebook.com/grincom

http://www.twitter.com/grin_com

PERFORMANCE ANALYSIS OF PROACTIVE REACTIVE AND HYBRID ROUTING PROTOCOLS CONSIDERING LINK SNR VALUE USING QUALNET

[*1]Ms. A. Sivasankari, [*2]Mrs. S. Sudarvizhi and, [3]N.Kalaiselvi

[1,2]*Department of Computer Science, D.K.M College for Women, Vellore, TamilNadu, India*

ABSTRACT

Ad-hoc network is a concept in computer communications, which means that users wanting to communicate with each other from a temporary network, without any form of centralized administration. Each node participating in the network acts both as host and router and must therefore be willing to forward packets for other nodes. For this purpose, a routing protocol is needed. Routing protocols in MANET such as OLSR-INRIA, DSR and ZRP finds out the path between a given sources destination node pair without considering the reliability of the links in the selected path. Some links in MANET are unreliable due to interference from transmissions from adjacent links, ambient noise system noise, jamming signals from intruder nodes all of which results in low throughput, packet delivery ratio, high jitter and end-to-end delay. In our work, we use Signal-to-Noise Ratio (SNR) as a measure of the link reliability. We propose modified secure version of the of three protocols namely OLSR-INRIA, DSR & ZRP coined as SOLSR-INRIA , SDSR, & SZRP which takes into account the link SNR value as a measure of link reliability in addition to the other parameters as in the original method in the route discovery phase. QualNet network simulator have been extensively used to evaluate the performance of our modified secure routing protocol over two different network scenarios consisting of 52 and 72 mobile nodes respectively considering random waypoint (RWP) mobility model. The results indicate high throughput, high packet delivery ratio and low jitter and end-to-end delay in comparison to the original protocols which do not account for wireless links reliability.

Keywords:- SOLSR-INRIA, SDSR, SZRP, SNR, RWP, Throughput, Packet Delivery Ratio, Jitter, Reliability, Network Topology, Qualnet.

1. INTRODCUTION

A Mobile Ad-hoc Network (MANET) consists of a number of mobile battery powered energy constraint nodes communicating with each other in single or multiple hops over wireless links. They are temporary and infrastructure less without any central controller. Every node generates its own data traffic and cooperatively forwards others which are not in direct communication range of each other i.e. acts both as an end terminal and router. Due to the mobility and dynamic addition/deletion of nodes, topology changes frequently and on-demand routing protocols *are* required. MANETs should be capable of handling these topology changes through network reconfigurations. Routing protocols for MANET should be adaptive to the topology changes and be capable of discovering new routes when old routes becomes invalid due to such change. The number of nodes in MANET changes with time so the routing protocols should be scalable.

A mobile ad hoc network is a collection of wireless mobile nodes that are dynamically and arbitrarily located in such a manner that the interconnections between nodes are capable of changing on a continual basis. There are some unique characteristics of mobile ad hoc networks.

1.1 ROUTING PROTOCOLS

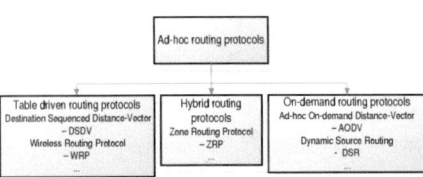

Fig 1: Routing Protocol

- **Table driven:** Every node in the network maintains complete routing information about the network by periodically updating the routing table. Thus, when a node needs to send data packets, there is no delay for discovering the route throughout the network. This kind of routing protocols roughly works the same way as that of routing protocols for wired networks.

- **Source initiated (or demand driven):** In this type of routing, a node simply maintains routes to active destination that it needs to send data. The routes to active destinations will expire after some time of inactivity, during which the network is not being used.

- **Hybrid:** This type of routing protocols combines features of the above two categories. Nodes belonging to a particular geographical region or within a certain distance from a concerned node are said to be in the routing zone and use table driven routing protocol. Communication between nodes in different zones will rely on the on-demand or source-initiated protocols.

This type of protocols maintains fresh lists of destinations and their routes by periodically distributing routing tables throughout the network. The main disadvantages of such algorithms are:

- Respective amount of data for maintenance.
- Slow reaction on restructuring and failures.

2. OLSR-INRIA, DSR AND ZRP
2.1 OLSR-INRIA
The Optimized Link State Routing (OLSR) protocol was designed by the French National Institute for Research in Computer Science and Control (INRIA) for mobile ad-hoc networks. It is a proactive routing protocol that employs an efficient link state packet forwarding mechanism called multipoint relaying on its way to optimize pure link state routing protocol. There is a two way optimization. One by reducing the size of the control packets and other by reducing the number of links that are used for forwarding link state packets. The reduction in the size of the link state packets is made by declaring only a subset of the links in the link state updates which are assigned the responsibility of packet forwarding known as Multipoint Relays. Periodic link state updates are facilitated by the optimization done by multipoint relaying facilities. No control packet is generated on the event of a link break or addition of a new link by the link state update mechanism which achieves higher efficiency when operating in a highly dense network.

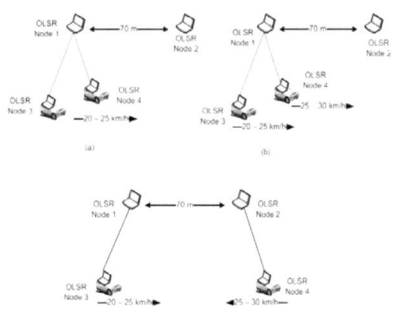

Fig 2: ROUTE OLSR.

2.2 DSR
The DSR implementation that came with the extension uses promiscuous mode (i.e. eavesdropping), which means that the protocol learns information from packets that it overhears. The question is how realistic this is in a real environment. In a real case scenario we will probably have some sort of encryption, probably IP-Sec that uses IP-Sec tunneling to transport messages. We have made some small change to DSR that makes it possible to turn the eavesdropping feature on and off. The parameters that are configurable for DSR are shown in These values are the values specified in the DSR draft and have not

been changed. The no propagating timeout is the time a node waits for a reply for a no propagating search. A no propagating search is a request that first goes to the neighbors. If the neighbors do not answer in this specified amount of a tune, a new request that will be forwarded by the neighbors will be sent. The send buffer in the DSR can hold 64 packets and the packets are allowed to stay in the buffer for 30 seconds

Parameter	Value
Time between retransmitted requests	500 ms
Size of source route header carrying n addresses	4n + 4 bytes
Timeout for no propagating search	30 ms
Time to hold packets awaiting routes	30 s

Table 1: Time Access Protocols

3 SYSTEM ANALYSES

Routing Characteristics	Proactive	Reactive	Hybrid
Routing structure	Both flat and hierarchical	Mostly flat, except CBRP	Mostly hierarchical
Route availability	Always available, if the nodes reachable	Determined when needed	Depends on the location of the destination
Traffic control	Usually high	Low	Mostly lower than proactive and reactive
Mobility handling effects	usually updates occurs based on mobility at fixed intervals	ABR introduced LBQ, AODV uses local route discovery	Usually more than one path may be available
Storage requirements	High	Usually lower than proactive protocols	Usually depends on the size of each cluster
Delay level	Some all routes are predetermined	Higher than proactive	For local destination small, since inter zone may be as large as reactive protocols.
Scalability level to perform efficient routing	Usually up to 100 nodes	Source routing protocols up to few 100 nodes point to point may scale higher	Designed for up to 1000 or more nodes

Table 2: Characteristics of Routing Protocols

3.1 ROUTING DEPENDABILITY IN AD HOC NETWORKS

- The effects of node misbehavior.
- Modeling adhoc networks.

There might be cases that the protocols that we have discussed cannot help out. For instance what if there are some nodes that do not want to cooperate? Or some other problems related proximity to each other. Some might behave as malicious and etc. Recall that in ad hoc networks, there is mobility, dynamic situations. In this part, our concern is Routing system.

Routing System – Definition

"A routing system delivers messages from a source node to a destination node by means of networked intermediate nodes (routers), which implement the functional process (routing) of identity resolution, path computation, and message forwarding."

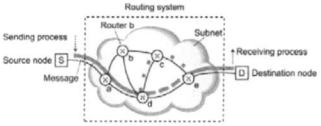

Fig 2.1: Node Distribution

3.2 NODE MISBEHAVIOR

A node in the middle may keep the message and not forward to package. It can affect the overall performance of the system. There are three different nodes.

1. Well-behaving nodes: that works, forwards the packet.
2. Malicious nodes: the ones that inject false information into messages or remove them completely from the network (blackholes).It has been proven that if the number of selfish nodes increases the packet loss in the network increases linearly as well. Besides that, in case of AODV, if there are many selfish nodes in the network we need to incerase the number of control messages (to keep the track of what is going on in the network , and reestablish route if a node does not forward the packet) . It results in increase of routing overhead. Selfish nodes: the ones that receives the packet but do not forward it.

3.3 ROUTING DEPENDABILITY PROBLEMS

Most ad hoc routing algorithms assume only well-behaving nodes to support multi-hop operation of the network. However if something goes wrong in between, everything can be affected in a negative way.

3.4 ROUTE DISCOVERY PHASE

The destination node unicasts the best route (the one received first) and caches the other routes for future use. A *route cache* is maintained at every node so that, whenever a node receives a route request and finds a route for the destination node in its own cache, it sends a RREP packet itself instead of broadcasting it further.

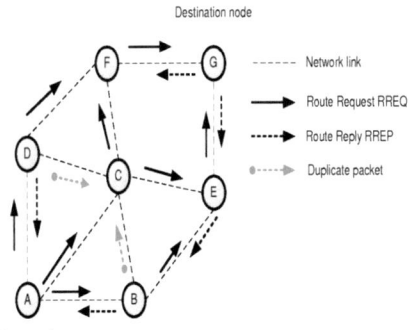

Fig 3: DSR Route Discovery

ROUTE MAINTENANCE

The route maintenance phase is carried out whenever there is a broken link between two nodes. A broken link can be detected by a node by either passively monitoring in promiscuous mode or actively monitoring the link. As shown in Figure 3.3, when a link break (F-G) happens, a route error packet (RERR) is sent by the intermediate node back to the originating node. The source node re-initiates the route discovery procedure to find a new route to the destination. It also removes any route entries it may have in its cache to that destination node. DSR benefits from source routing since the intermediate nodes do not need to maintain up-to-date routing information in order to route the packets that they receive. There is also no need for any periodic routing advertisement messages.

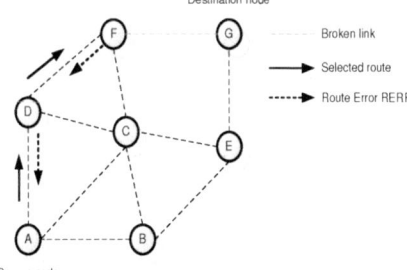

Fig 4: ROUTE MAINTENANCE

Availability guarantees the survivability of the network services despite attacks. A Denial-of-Service (DoS) is a potential threat at any layer of an ad hoc network. On the media access control layer, an adversary could jam the physical communication channels. On the network layer disruption of the routing operation may result in a partition of the network, rendering certain nodes inaccessible. On higher levels, an attacker could bring down high-level services like key management service.

Confidentiality ensures that certain information be never disclosed to unauthorized entities. It is of paramount importance to strategic or tactical military communications. Routing information must also remain confidential in some cases, because the information might be valuable for enemies to locate their targets in a battlefield.

Integrity ensures that a message that is on the way to the destination is never corrupted. A message could be corrupted because of channel noise or because of malicious attacks on the network.

Authentication enables a node to ensure the identity of the peer node. Without authentication, an attacker could masquerade as a normal node, thus gaining access to sensitive information.

Non-repudiation ensures that the originator of a message cannot deny that it is the real originator. Non-repudiation is important for detection and isolation of compromised nodes.

4. SIMULATION SCENARIO AND RESULTS

We have considered two different network scenarios with the first one having 52 nodes with 7 different source and destination pairs (Figure 6.1) and the second one having 72 nodes with 7 different source and destination pairs (Figure 6.2) respectively. Qualnet 4.5 network simulator is used to extensively simulate the above mentioned scenarios. We have taken the packet size to be 512 bytes. User Datagram Protocol (UDP) is used as the transport layer protocol and Constant Bit Rate (CBR) traffic is used as the application layer protocol applied between the source and destination. In the first scenario CBR traffic is applied between seven source destination node pairs namely (3, 40), (5, 38), (13, 47), (17, 49), (19, 46), (28, 35) and (39, 07) respectively as depicted in figure 1 over randomly deployed 52 nodes in the deployment area. In the second scenario similarly CBR traffic is applied between seven source destination node pairs namely (2, 39), (12, 30), (19, 27), (23, 41), (45, 31), (55, 29) and (65, 16) respectively as shown in figure 2 over randomly deployed 72 nodes in the deployment area. In both the scenarios Random Waypoint (RWP) mobility model is considered.

It gives a list of various simulation parameters. We have enhanced both security and throughput at the same reducing end-to-end delay and jitter in our proposed schemes. This can be attributed to the fact by taking only links with high SNR value we ensure reliability, increased throughput and security. Jamming and interfering signals from intruder or malicious nodes lowers a link's SNR ratio and provides a good indication about its reliability and security

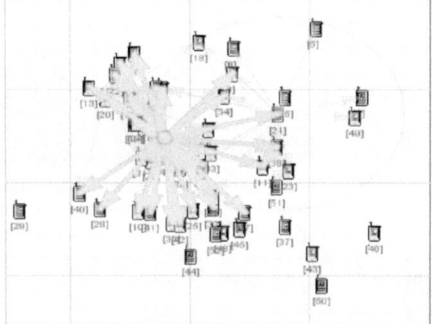

Fig 5: Network scenario comprising of 52 mobile nodes and 7 different source - destination traffic pairs.

Parameter	Value
Area	1500m X 1500m
Data Rate	2 Mbps
Packet Size	512 bytes.
Mobility Model	Random-Way Point
Physical Layer Radio Type	IEEE 802.11b,Abstract
MAC Protocol	IEEE 802.11
Antenna Model	Omni directional
Temperature	290 K
SNR Threshold	10 dB

Table 3: Simulation Area

Jitter measures the variability of delay of packets in the given stream, which is an important property for many applications (for example, streaming real-time applications). Ideally, packets should be delivered in a perfectly periodic fashion; however, even if the source generates an evenly spaced stream, unavoidable jitter is introduced by the network due to the variable queuing and propagation delays, and packets arrive at the destination with a wide range of inter-arrival times. The jitter increases at switches along the path of a connection due to many factors, such as conflicts with other packets wishing to use the same links, and nondeterministic propagation delay in the data-link layer. In our modified protocol average jitter decreases for SOLSR-INRIA, SDSR and as well as for SZRP. The results are shown in table 4. Fig 5.

In case of SOLSR-INRIA the Jitter is decreased by 52% for the first scenario and 67% for the second scenario. In case of SDSR the Jitter is decreased by 84% for the first scenario and 75% for the second scenario. As well as for SZRP the Jitter is decreased by 68% for the first scenario and 76% for the second scenario.

Throughput (In Sec)	52 Nodes Scenario	72 Nodes scenario
OLSR-INRIA	12.7	16.12
SOLSR-INRIA	17.1	30.5
DSR	39.5	29.5
SDSR	30.5	30.8
ZRP	4.2	6.2
SZRP	29.7	30.1

Table 4: Throughput

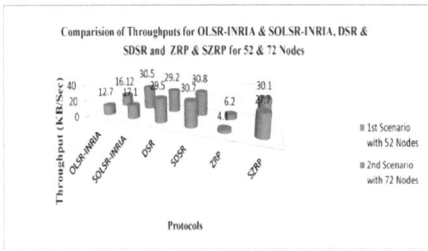

Fig 6: ThroughPut

Pause Time (seconds)	Packet Delivery Fraction (%)	Normalized Routing Load
DSR	68.41%	1.72
OLSR	54.70%	2.58
AODV	93.45%	0.56
SAODV	92.00%	0.98
ZRP	75.00%	1.01

Table 5: Packet Delivery Ratio

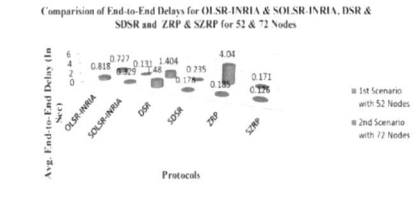

Fig 7: End to End Delay

PERFORMANCE COMPARISON

Parameters	AODV	DSR	ZRP
Hop Count	Normal	Very High	Medium
Possible Routes Selected	Less	More	Medium
Congestion	Medium	More	Medium
UpdatePackets/ Messages Received	Almost Same	Almost Same	Very Low
Error Messages	More	Less	Medium
Routing Scheme	Reactive	Reactive	Hybrid
Routing Overhead	Low	Low	Medium
Throughput	High	Low	Medium
Delay of Time	Low	High	Medium

Table 6: Comparison

5. EXPERIENTIAL RESULT

First, the four protocols are used in a being environment, in which there is no network attack, in order to collect baseline values for the metrics. The differences amongst baseline values of the protocols are also discussed in order to get better understanding of each protocol's operation.

Second, each of the protocols is evaluated in various simulated malicious environments. The collected metrics are compared with the respective baseline values, in order to assess the impact of a particular network attack on the protocol operation. Based on the results we've collected, we conclude that, in all the malicious environments, normal routing protocols (DSR and AODV) can not guarantee to deliver data to the destinations as well as in the benign environments. In other words, the data is redirected or discarded due to the attacks on the routing protocol. When the number of malicious nodes increases, the number of received data packets decreases. For the secure versions of the routing protocols (OLSR and SAODV), they are designed to detect the changes in routing packets; hence, even under attacks, they are still able to deliver the data to the destinations. However, under specific attacks like route fabrication attack for OLSR and impersonation attack for SAODV, the protocol requires the existence of a specific security mechanism, in order to maintain the normal operation. That is the key management center for SAODV and the secure cached routes for OLSR.

Decreases considerably as compared to OLSR-INRIA, DSR and ZRP in both the scenarios. The modified protocols avoid malicious nodes and noisy links by choosing the highest SNR path which increases overall network reliability. Random Waypoint (RWP).I have implemented two secure routing protocols, OLSR and SAODV, based on their respective underlying protocols, DSR and AODV.The attack models are used to make malicious wireless nodes and create various malicious environments, in which the performance of DSR, AODV, OLSR, and SAODV are evaluated.

SCENERIES

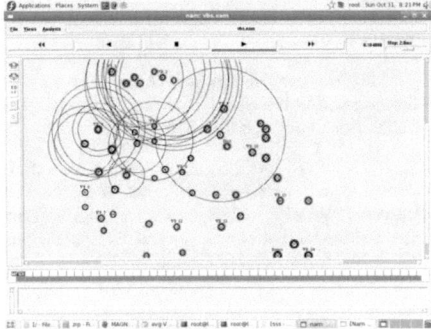

Fig 8: Node Distribution

We have measured end to end throughput in Kbits/sec for each source destination pair over both the network scenarios. A high individual and average throughput is observed in all the cases by the modified protocols. The result obtained can be attributed to the fact that due to the selection of the path having highest SNR value the impact of interference and jamming signals are less and path bandwidth is increased which is reflected as higher throughput that is desirable for almost every envisaged application of MANET. A considerable improvement in average throughput is observed in both the scenario for all routing protocol.

The overall end to end delay is reduced which is an important QoS in applications such as video streaming, live telecast and others. Fig 6 shows the end to end delay for scenario 1 and scenario 2 as well. A significant reduction in average end to end delay is observed which makes this type of modified protocol suitable for video streaming operations.

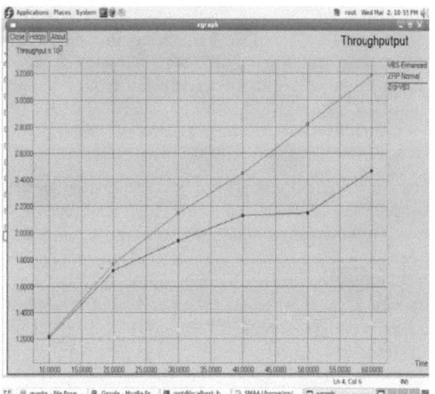

Fig 9: Throughput

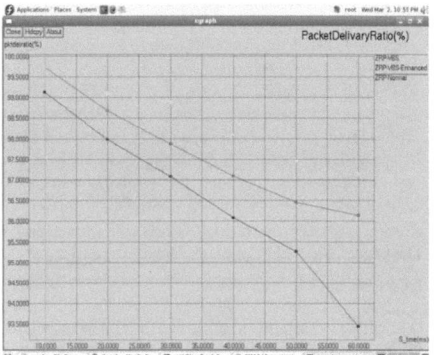

Fig 10: Packet Delivery Ratio

6. CONCLUSION

From the simulation results it can be concluded that for SOLSR-INRIA, SDSR and SZRP average throughput increases while average end-to-end delay and jitter decreases considerably as compared to OLSR-INRIA, DSR and ZRP in both the scenarios. The modified protocols avoid malicious nodes and noisy links by choosing the highest SNR path which increases overall network reliability. Random Waypoint (RWP) mobility model is considered as it encompasses most of the envisaged application areas of MANETs. We have extensively simulated our methods using QualNet 4.5 network simulator. As a future work other mobility models and data traffic might be considered. Intrusion detection methods may be incorporated in the route discovery phase of OLSR-INRIA, DSR and ZRP for detection of malicious nodes to enhance network reliability.

In this thesis, I have implemented two secure routing protocols, OLSR and SAODV, based on their respective underlying protocols, DSR and AODV, in the OPNET simulation environment. I have also simulated four popular network attack models that exploit the weakness of the protocols. The attack models are used to make malicious wireless nodes and create various malicious environments, in which the performance of DSR, AODV, OLSR, and SAODV are evaluated. With three different attack models for each of the protocols, and with the number of malicious nodes varying from one to five, totally 65 scenarios are created to evaluate the four protocols.

The ultimate goal of a routing protocol is to efficiently deliver the network data to the destinations; therefore, two metrics, Packet Delivery Fraction (PDF) and Normalized Routing Load (NRL), are used to evaluate the protocols. In order to get the accurate experimental results, each scenario is run eleven times in order to calculate the average value for the two evaluation metrics. Through the collected evaluation metrics from the various scenarios, the impacts of attacks upon the routing protocols are then studied. The procedure is summarized below:

REFERENCES

[1] T.H Clausen, G.Hansen, L.Christensen, G. Behrmann, " **The Optimised Link State Routing Protocol Evaluation Through Experiments and Simulations**", Proceedings of IEEE Symposium on Wireless Personal Mobile Communications, 2001, September 2001.

[2] D.B Johnson, D.A. Maltz, "**Dynamic Source Routing in Ad Hoc Wireless Networks**", Mobile Computing, Kluwer Academic Publishers, 1996, vol. 353, pp. 153-181.

[3] D. Sivakumar, B. Suseela, R. Varadharajan, "**A Survey of Routing Algorithms for MANET**", IEEE International Conference on Advances in Engineering, Science and Management (ICAESM), March 30-31, 2012, pp. 625- 640. Available in IEEE Explore.

4] V.Jha, K. Khetarpal, M.Sharma, "**A Survey of Nature inspired Routing Algorithms for MANETs**", IEEE 3rd International Conference on Electronics, Computing Technology (ICECT), April 8-10, 2011, pp. 1-4. Available in IEEE Explore.

[5] S.Weber, J.G Andrews, N. Jindal, "**An Overview of Transmission Capacity of Wireless Networks**", IEEE Transactions on Communication, vol. 58, Issue. 12, 2010, pp. 3593-3604.

[6] Royer E M, Toh C K, "**A review of current routing protocols for Adhoc mobile wireless networks**" IEEE Journal of Personal Communications, Dec. 2006, vol. 6(2), pp. 46- 55.

[7] Z.J Haas, "**The Routing Algorithm for the Reconfigurable Wireless Networks**", Proceedings of ICUPC 1997, vol. 2, pp. 562-566, October 1997.

[8] P. Nand, and S.C. Sharma, "**Performance study of Broadcast based Mobile Ad hoc Routing Protocols AODV, DSR and DYMO**", Proc. International Journal of Security and Its Applications, Vol. 5, No. 1, January, 2011, pp. 53-64.